A Day in the Life: Grassland Animals

Ostrich

Louise Spilsbury

Raintree

www.raintreepublishers.co.uk
Visit our website to find out
more information about
Raintree books.

To order:

☎ Phone 0845 6044371
🖹 Fax +44 (0) 1865 312263
🖳 Email myorders@raintreepublishers.co.uk

Customers from outside the UK please telephone +44 1865 312262

Raintree is an imprint of Capstone Global Library Limited,
a company incorporated in England and Wales having its
registered office at 7 Pilgrim Street, London, EC4V 6LB
– Registered company number: 6695582

Edited by Dan Nunn, Rebecca Rissman, Catherine Veitch
   and Nancy Dickmann
Designed by Philippa Jenkins
Picture research by Mica Brancic
Originated by Capstone Global Library
Printed and bound in China by South China Printing
   Company Ltd

ISBN 978 1 406 21900 5 (hardback)
15 14 13 12 11
10 9 8 7 6 5 4 3 2 1

ISBN 978 1 406 21904 3 (paperback)
16 15 14 13 12
10 9 8 7 6 5 4 3 2 1

British Library Cataloguing in Publication Data
Spilsbury, Louise.
Ostrich. -- (A day in the life. Grassland animals)
598.5'24-dc22
A full catalogue record for this book is available from the
British Library.

Acknowledgements
We would like to thank the following for permission to
reproduce photographs: Alamy pp. 6 (© Robert Fried), 10
(© MNS Photo), 12 (© Imagebroker/Bernd Zoller), 13 (©
Lana Sundman), 19 (© Juniors Bildarchiv); Ardea p. 16 (©
J. L. Mason); FLPA p. 17 (Sunset); iStockphoto p. 23 cheetah
(© BostjanT); Nature Picture Library p. 22 (© Tony Heald);
Shutterstock pp. 4 (© Urosr), 5 (© Eric Isselée), 7, 23 female,
23 male (© Four Oaks), 9, 23 grassland (© Mdd), 11 (©
Mogens Trolle), 14 (© Smeyf), 15 (© John Carnemolla), 18,
23 mongoose (© Palko72), 20 (© Gallofoto), 21 (© Hallam
Creations), 23 hyena (© Antonio Jorge Nunes), 23 insect
(© kd2).

Cover photograph of a close-up portrait of an ostrich
reproduced with permission of Shutterstock (© Petr Vaclavek).
Back cover photographs of (left) an ostrich with eggs
reproduced with permission of Shutterstock (© Eric Isselée)
and (right) ostrich chicks reproduced with permission of FLPA
(Sunset).

We would like to thank Michael Bright for his invaluable help
in the preparation of this book.

The author would like to dedicate this book to her nephew and
niece, Ben and Amelie: "I wrote these books for animal lovers
like you. I hope you enjoy them." Aunty Louise.

Contents

Some words are in bold, **like this**. You can find out what they mean by looking in the glossary.

What is an ostrich?

An ostrich is a big bird that has wings but cannot fly.

The ostrich is the largest bird in the world.

Ostriches lay bigger eggs than any other bird.

An ostrich egg is as big as a medium-sized melon!

What do ostriches look like?

Ostriches have a long neck and legs, and are taller than most men.

They have small heads but their eyes are as big as cricket balls!

Ostriches have long fluffy feathers on their back and wings.

Males have black and white feathers and **females** have mostly brown feathers.

Where do ostriches live?

key: ⬛ = where ostriches live

Ostriches live in parts of central and southern Africa.

They mostly live in places called **grasslands**.

In these grasslands the land is mostly covered in grasses.

Most days it is hot and dry, but in some months it rains a lot.

What do ostriches do during the day?

In the mornings and afternoons ostriches feed.

On days when it gets very hot they rest in the middle of the day.

Sometimes ostriches rub their bodies in dust.

This helps to keep their feathers in good shape.

What do ostriches eat?

food

Ostriches eat grasses and other plants, and sometimes **insects** too.

Ostriches only swallow when they have a big lump of food in their throat!

Ostriches also eat sand and small stones.

These help the birds to grind up the food that they swallow.

In the day, ostriches usually walk about slowly.

They hold their heads up high to look out for danger.

Ostriches cannot fly but they can run quickly if they spot trouble.

Ostriches can run twice as fast as a human!

Where do ostriches lay eggs?

egg

Female ostriches lay their eggs together in a shared nest.

Females keep eggs warm and safe during the day, and **males** take over at night.

Ostrich chicks are striped so they are hard to see among the grasses in the day.

When it is hot they hide from the sun under their parents' wings.

Which animals hunt ostriches?

mongoose

Mongooses and some other animals eat ostrich eggs and chicks.

Ostrich parents watch their eggs and chicks carefully to keep them safe.

Cheetahs, lions, leopards, wild dogs, and **hyenas** hunt adult ostriches.

Ostriches escape by running away or kicking these animals with their strong legs!

What do ostriches do at night?

Ostriches sleep at night.

They sleep sitting down on the ground.

At night it can get cold in the **grasslands** where ostriches live.

To keep warm, an ostrich wraps its wings around itself like a blanket!

Ostrich body map

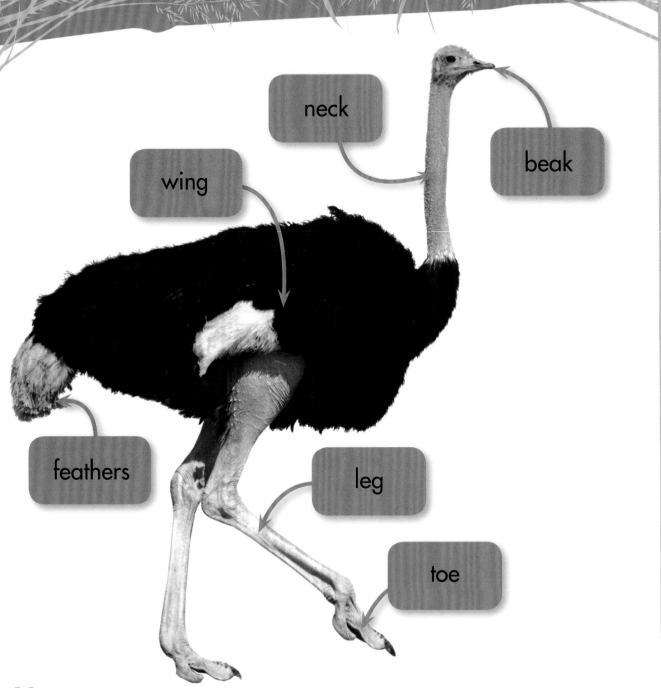

neck

wing

beak

feathers

leg

toe

Glossary

 cheetah large, spotted wild cat. A cheetah lives in Africa.

 female animal that can become a mother when it is grown up

 grassland land where mostly grasses grow

 hyena wild animal that mostly lives in grasslands in Africa. It looks like a dog.

 insect small animal with six legs. Ants, beetles, and bees are insects.

male animal that can become a father when it is grown up

 mongoose wild animal that lives in Asia and Africa. It looks like a weasel.

Find out more

Books

Flightless Birds, Norman Barrett (Franklin Watts, 1991)
Ostriches (New Naturebooks), Thane Maynard
  (Child's World, 2006)

Websites

http://animals.nationalgeographic.com/animals/birds/ostrich.
  html
http://www.bbc.co.uk/nature/species/Ostrich

Index